Forever Grateful

Inspirational Christian Poetry
by
Christine V Mitchell

Forever Grateful
by Christine V Mitchell

First published 2014

Written, compiled and prepared for publishing by the author.

Interior images (originally) by
kozzi.com; morguefile.com

Scripture quotations taken from the Holy Bible
King James Version (KJV)

Copyright registered with Copyright House

ISBN-10: 149369247X
ISBN-13: 978-1493692477

DEDICATION

I dedicate this book to God
- the source of my inspiration -
to my family and friends
and to you, dear reader.
Be blessed.

Touch my hands, let them write
precious words that bring light,
that may shine in the darkness
and dead of the night.
May Your love ever flow
through the ink of this pen,
from a heart of thanksgiving, Lord,
again and again.

Christine V Mitchell

CONTENTS

ACKNOWLEDGEMENTS

Firstly, I give praise and thanks to God for His inspiration. Without Him, none of this would have been possible and it is my prayer that He will be glorified through this work.

Special thanks to my loving husband, Frederick, and to our children, for their patience and support during my long hours at the computer in preparing this work, and for their help and encouragement in the final proof-reading and editing.

Thanks to my cousin-in-law Rev Lydia Woodson-Sloley (Founder and Senior Pastor of Life in Its Poetic Form Christian Ministries Inc) for her wonderful words of advice, encouragement and support.

I would also like to thank Sandra Stoner-Mitchell, Judith K Wood and Kat Mizelle for their helpful advice and support.

*"My soul shall make her boast in the
Lord: the humble shall hear thereof, and
be glad. O magnify the Lord with me, and
let us exalt His Name together"*
(Psalm 34: 2-3 KJV)

INTRODUCTION

"Forever Grateful" is a collection of 40 inspirational poems of faith, my first book of poetry. It is full of poetic moments of reflection, expressions of encouragement and appreciation of the love and goodness of God. Each chapter begins with devotional thoughts and many of the poems (which are both rhymed and free verse) are accompanied by Biblical references. This was part of a larger collection, but I decided to extract a small portion for my first book.

The writing of many poems is something I never would have dreamed and I give God all the glory for this work. Having a relationship with God through Jesus Christ is my greatest joy and I am truly thankful for the opportunity to share this through poetry. I am continually amazed when I think about how wonderful He is and often find inspirations flowing during prayer, worship or in the midst of almost any activity.

My purpose in writing this book is to help uplift and inspire readers through expressions of what He means to me. As you read and meditate on the words, you may find that some echo your own experience or express your heart.

Wherever you are in your journey of life or faith, it's my hope and prayer that these poems will be a source of blessing and encouragement.

-   *Christine Mitchell*

Chapter 1

Adoration

Devotional Thoughts

As we think back over our lives and take the time to acknowledge and appreciate the goodness of God, it's in thankfulness that we can develop an attitude of gratitude that prepares our hearts and opens the way for more of His blessings.

"Bless the Lord, O my soul:
and all that is within me,
bless His holy Name.
Bless the Lord, O my soul,
and forget not all His benefits"
(Psalm 103: 1-2 KJV)

I'll SING A MELODY

I'll sing to You a melody
of love divine, for deep within
this heart of mine is gratitude, O Lord.
You lifted me when hope was gone,
You helped me stand and kept me strong.
Your peace within, no money could afford.

Although sometimes in life I've failed,
Your precious love has still prevailed;
it reaches high and low, to great and small.
To the deepest places in my heart
it makes it ways and never parts;
I marvel at the wonder of it all.

Wide as the ocean, ever strong,
Your love forgives, Your love lives on.
To broken lives and hearts, it is the cure.
Its melody I'll always sing.
Your love to me is everything,
embracing all mankind forevermore!

--o0o--

IT'S ALL ABOUT YOU

I love You Lord, You're my inspiration,
the centre of all my appreciation.

You're good and perfect in all Your ways
and for this, I just want to give You praise.

To be more like You, Lord, each day
is my heart's desire, on this upward way.

You're my life and my hope, enduringly;
I need not struggle, for it's not about me.

It's all about trusting alone in Your grace.
It's all about giving You rightful place.

It's all about walking with You as my Guide
and letting Your word within me abide.

It's all about letting Your Spirit control,
for You are the One who makes me whole.

There are prayers to pray, there are needs I see.
But within I joy, for You live in me.

When You're in control, there is peace and rest;
when it's all about You, I am truly blessed!

--oOo—

JOY OF MY LIFE

As I come into Your presence Lord
in need again of grace;
You melt my heart dear Jesus with
the beauty of Your face.
Your warm touch is so precious,
only You can satisfy
the longing of my heart O Lord
whenever You are nigh.

To think about Your goodness gives me
joy deep down within.
I thank You for Your mercy and
forgiveness of my sins.
Forever may I worship You
and songs of gladness raise.
From dawn until the sunset,
You are worthy of my praise!

"In Thy presence is fullness of joy;
at Thy right hand there are pleasures forevermore"
(Psalm 16:11b KJV)

--o0o—

BE THANKFUL

Let's offer up a sound of praise
to the Lord above, each and every day,
with grateful hearts of jubilation,
thankfulness and appreciation;

for things around us, great and small;
by His own Word, He made them all.
Beautiful sights we take for granted;
awesome colour His hand has painted.

Sights and sounds both far and near;
blessings He gives that bring us cheer.
Things we have that brighten our lives;
family and friends that help us thrive.

Tests and trials that make us strong
and faith to endure, however long.
What do we have that we didn't receive?
Even a measure of faith to believe.

Thank You Lord for the joy You bring.
We give You praise for everything!

--oOo--

PRECIOUS SAVIOUR

May the perfume of Your love
and the sweetness of Your grace
fill our hearts Lord from above,
bring a smile upon each face.

May the kindness that You show
that brings warmth to many hearts,
as a soft and gentle glow,
be the kindness we impart.

May the river of Your peace
overflow and bring elation
and the joy of You increase
through the blessings of salvation.

Precious Saviour, You are awesome!
You are brighter than the sun!
May the preciousness of knowing You
be felt by everyone!

--o0o—

YOU'RE EVERYTHING

You are the sum of all that I admire.
A glimpse of You means all the world to me.
To worship and adore You lifts me higher;
how wonderful that You should think of me!

A million moons and thousand suns combined
could not outshine the brilliance of Your love.
You transform and bring peace to troubled minds
and shower abundant mercy from above.

You're the gold that no-one ever could afford,
yet You came down to give Your life for us;
You are so precious, Jesus Christ, our Lord,
a faithful Friend in Whom we put our trust.

O who can stand before Your holiness?
Where sin abounds, no-one could dare draw near,
but You have made the way to save and bless
so we can come before You, free of fear.

Exalted are You, Lord, forevermore;
all heaven sings Your praise eternally.
You are the sum of all that we adore,
and all that we could ever desire to be!

--oOo--

ALL THE GLORY IS YOURS

Whatever good that I may do on earth,
dear Lord, it's all because You gave me worth.
The glory, Lord, belongs to You always;
forever, I will give You all the praise.

It's all because Your precious light of love
shone in my heart one day, from heaven above,
and all because You brought me to this place,
I stand because of Your redeeming grace.

I thank You for the mercy that You show
and for the many blessings You bestow,
so undeserved, but yet You give to me -
it's all because You love eternally.

Each day, my God, Your goodness I can see
and everything I have You gave to me.
The glory, Lord, belongs to You always.
Forever, I will give You all the praise.

--oOo--

DEEPER AND HIGHER

Much deeper in the ocean of Your love,
my soul desires to go with You each day;
as eagles spread their wings to fly above,
may I reach higher heights, Lord, as I pray.

O may my eyes be open, Lord, to see
the light of glory of shining from Your face,
and may I feel Your cool refreshing rain
now fall in showers of renewing grace.

To understand the greatness of Your peace
is something that we cannot comprehend,
but I am grateful when I can release
my load in prayer to You, my greatest Friend.

O let Your all-consuming Fire burn.
You are my soul's desire, for You I yearn.

--oOo--

Chapter 2

Expressions of His Love

Devotional Thoughts

Sometimes life's journey takes a path we didn't expect. At times, we may feel that God is far away, when He's so very near. The Psalmist, David, said

> "If I take the wings of the morning,
> and dwell in the uttermost parts of the sea;
> even there shall Thy hand lead me,
> and Thy right hand shall hold me."
> (Psalm 139: 9-10 KJV)

MINE IS THE LOVE

Mine is the love that stands through time,
a love that never fails.
Upon the cross, My love lived on,
although My hands were nailed.
The pangs of death and hell could not
prevent love's burning fire.
To see you whole again has been
My Father's great desire.

I rose again, for death could not
obliterate this love,
and now the way is open to
My Father's throne above.
Each day that passes by, I see
the longing of your heart.
It's My desire to comfort you
and My love to impart.

You're precious and I long to give you
everlasting peace,
and reassure you daily that
My mercies never cease.
Mine is the love that stands through time,
O come to Me, dear soul.
Receive My precious love, sublime,
that never will grow old.

--o0o--

LOOK NO FURTHER

Look no further, child of Mine,
though your friends may turn away,
You can trust My love divine -
I'll be there at the end of the day;
just as I was in the morning light,
when you saw the clear blue skies,
when around you things looked bright
and it was easy to arise.
Even in the twilight hour
when the changing scenes unfold,
My love is like a lasting flower,
never can My love grow old.
Every moment that passes by,
thoughts of you are on My mind.
My love for you is the reason why
I gave My Son, so you would find
peace, contentment, joy divine –
light to guide you on your way.
Look no further, child of Mine,
these blessings can be yours today.

--o0o—

THE FATHER'S HEART

The heart of the Father is one that forgives.
His heart of compassion says, "Come .. and live.
I know you've been wandering, then lost your way;
I know you have felt I was too far away.

At My banqueting table, I've kept you a place.
You may not feel able, but trust in My grace.
I'm your heavenly Father and I understand.
I'll take you there, if you'll hold My hand.

If hope for tomorrow seems clouded by grief,
I'm right here to comfort your soul and bring peace.
No more do you ever need struggle alone.
I love you, forever - please come back home".

--o0o--

YOU'RE VERY SPECIAL

You're very special.
You are God's prize.
You're in His heart.
Do you realise?
Made for a purpose,
uniquely designed;
each day, each hour,
you're on His mind.

Though darkness may hide
His light from you,
His eyes of love
will still shine through.
The mists and shadows
will all flee away,
for His light will shine
more brightly than day.

Your peace within
is His heart's desire;
His love for you
is a burning fire.
He stopped at nothing
when He gave His Son,
the Lord Jesus Christ,
for everyone.

His purpose on earth
His plan, His goal
is to make you complete -
body, spirit and soul.
Because you are special
in the Father's eyes,
the devil is angry
and often he tries

to throw up a tantrum
and snare your path,
then sits back and watches
the great aftermath.
But don't let him fool you,
whatever you do;
always remember that
GOD LOVES YOU!

--o0o--

THERE'S HOPE

Take the strain off your mind,
relax and unwind
and give yourself a break.

Don't be in a hurry,
just give your worries
a rest, for your own sake.

The sun will shine brighter,
the load will get lighter,
just hold on a while, you will see.

There's hope for tomorrow
and all of your sorrow
will soon be a memory.

There may come a day,
it may come your way
when someone special you'll meet,

with arms open wide,
who'll stand by your side,
for whom your heart will beat.

Don't ever give up
when the going gets tough
and friends are hard to find.

There's Someone above
with a heart of love,
He has you on His mind!

--oOo—

INSEPARABLE LOVE

Walls are never too high,
valleys are never too deep,
no powers that be in the skies,
no sorrows that cause us to weep.

No earthly thing great or small
or mysteries of heaven above,
things present or things to come
can separate us from Your love.

Of this I am fully persuaded;
forever, this truth I will hold,
Your love, Lord, has never faded -
it's a love that will never grow old.

--oOo—

(Based on Romans 8: 38-39 KJV)

GOD KNOWS

Through life, we walk the hills and plains,
and sometimes face a mountain;
we often need more strength again
from Christ the living Fountain.

Our Saviour walked the road before,
He knows the storms we face.
He says to us, "I am the Door"
and gives to us more grace.

Again, He says, "I am the Way,
the Truth and I'm the Life".
His peace within our hearts today
can calm all inner strife.

Temptation He has overcome,
destroying Satan's power;
through Christ, the victory is won,
He'll help us in that hour.

The words He speaks, He will not brake.
He'll always see us through;
He knows the journey that we take,
through Him we'll make it too!

--o0o--

ABIDING LOVE

If all through life I'd never known His love,
the gold that shines on dark and cloudy days,
that lifts me up and helps me rise above,
to see beyond the fog or misty haze.

The jewel may have been a broken dream,
a cherished hope forever kept inside;
at best, I may have glimpsed a bright sunbeam,
until my eyes were really opened wide.

This love has kept me sailing on the sea,
for winds and waves can never stop its power;
through everything it reaches out to me
and keeps me steady every passing hour.

Lord, may this love, just like a river, flow,
Your love, O God, which brightens up our way,
so someone else may truly come to know
Your joy within, to cheer their hearts today.

--oOo--

JUST BECAUSE

I have a reason
whatever the season
to hold my head up high.
I count .. I'm someone
just like everyone
below Your fathomless sky.

Not of noble birth,
to You I'm of worth -
that matters most of all.
You came into my heart,
gave me a new start,
in prayer, it's Your Name I call.

You're high but came low,
just so I could know
a love – unlike any other.
In You, I'm complete, as I sit at Your feet.
You are closer to me than a brother.

… From my heart, I just want to say …

Thank you, Lord Jesus
that it's not about achieving,
but all about believing ..
.. that You're there - that You care,
just because

YOU ARE LOVE
personified

--o0o--

YOU INSPIRE ME

When I pause to think about
how much Your love is real,
I love to pen the thoughts within,
Your love gives me this zeal.

Moments of each day go by
when You inspire in me
appreciation of Who You are
in life and things I see.

You are the Morning Light, O Lord,
that shines and beautifies;
Your way is perfect, holy and pure.
You help me to be wise.

You're my Pillow and Comforter,
in You I find true rest.
You cover me with warmth and love,
in You I'm truly blessed.

You're the Judge of all my thoughts.
Your word brings light and truth,
correcting me, protecting me,
Your word renews my youth.

You're the Shepherd of my soul
Who never lets me stray.
Beside still waters, I'm restored.
You gently lead the way.

You're the Captain of my ship,
my Anchor in the storm.
When winds and waves come rushing by,
You help my ship stay firm.

You're my Life, my Hope, my Joy
in everything I do.
Dear Lord, these words are just a small
expression of love for You

--oOo—

YOU SHINE!

In You, my soul can feel at ease
when life's a rushing pace;
when busy thoughts just never cease,
You give me time and space

to recollect myself and brush
aside all earthly care,
to gaze upon Your loveliness,
refresh my soul in prayer.

You cleanse my soul from deep within
as I, in full surrender
confess to You my faults and sins,
I feel Your love, so tender.

A closer friend, I have not found
for there is none like You.
I bless You Lord, for all around
Your love shines through and through!

--oOo—

CHORDS OF LOVE

Your love is like the sweetest melody,
its music is a gentle flowing stream;
within my heart, an endless rhapsody,
for You're the sum of all my hopes and dreams.

If I could search the world, I'd never find
a greater love than Yours, so pure and free,
or peace that brings contentment to the mind,
or joy that gives new strength, dear Lord, to me.

May chords of love flow daily from my heart.
O let me be an instrument for You,
so the music of Your love they will impart
and melodies arise in others too.

--o0o--

CENTRE OF MY JOY

From the heavens, Love looked down,
left His glorious robe and crown
to pave the way for all of humankind.

Jesus Christ, the sacrifice -
for one and all He gave His life,
all because God had us on His mind.

Mercy looked beyond my shame
and lovingly called out my name,
saying "I have come to give you life".

Forgiveness came with open arms,
enveloped my soul with calm
and took away the inner doubts and strife.

Happiness evaded me,
until I came to Calvary
and looked upon the face of Him Who died.

Freedom broke the bars of sin
when I opened up to Him
and in my soul new tears of joy I cried.

By His grace, I walk this road,
thankful for the love He showed;
the peace He gives me, nothing can destroy.

Strength within, He gives to me
and words of life that set me free.
He's my hope, the centre of my joy!

--o0o--

ONE THING STANDS SURE

Thunderstorms may follow clouds of grey,
crisp winter snow may fall each day,
winds of change may re-arrange,
things may often look strange,
but one thing stands sure,
nought can obscure
Your love that
shines as
gold!
**

Chapter 3

Gratitude

Devotional Thoughts

When we've done something for someone and they've expressed their appreciation, we feel good. The gratitude expressed may be even greater if the person felt undeserving. It brings pleasure to the heart of God too when we are thankful. We can develop a heart of thankfulness in response to His mercy and grace, and His many blessings, both great and small.

"And one of them, when he saw that he was healed,
turned back, and with a loud voice glorified God,"
(Luke 17:15 KJV)

"In everything give thanks:
for this is the will of God in Christ Jesus concerning you"
(1 Thessalonians 5: 18 KJV)

BECAUSE OF YOU I STAND

When just a babe, I never knew what life would hold,
just how my life without my mother would unfold.
I was too young to realise she was not there,
that I would miss her tender arms of love and care.

How often have I wished she was alive today.
I cannot turn the hands of time, there is no way.
I know that she is in a place of rest with You
and I am grateful, Lord, for all You've brought me through.

I'm thankful for the care within those early years,
for all who helped look after me and dried my tears;
for a wise and loving father who did all he could,
for helping me to stand, though oft misunderstood.

Throughout the years, dear Lord, I know that You were there.
You've kept me sailing on the sea and heard my prayer.
I know that I am standing, all because You came
into my life one day and I am not ashamed.

Though waves and billows sometimes try to flood my soul,
the comfort of Your Spirit always makes me whole.
You brought me from afar and kept me through Your love.
You give me strength each day, as I look up above.

From deep inside my heart, O Lord, I can't express
how precious, Lord, You are to me – I feel so blessed!

--o0o--

SIMPLY GRATEFUL

For trials faced,
through loss and pain,
I thank You Lord
for peace again.
Your mercy shows
in ways divine,
Your words of life
renew my mind.

Along my path
from day to day,
You're always near
to hear me pray.
Your brilliance shines
in all You do.
I'm simply grateful -
I love You!

--oOo—

THANK YOU FOR MY FAMILY

I thank You, dear Lord, for my family,
for the joys that we share together.
Like a tree that has grown to new heights,
they are there, through all kinds of weather.

For the music of laughter and sharing
of blessings in all different ways,
there is so much to thank You for;
You alone deserve all the praise.

The bonding of love You have given us
is a strong and enduring glue.
Through the years, it has grown even stronger,
through the love that comes from You.

From a long way, O Lord, You have brought us
and have kept us by Your grace.
I thank You so much for my family,
who I'll cherish and always embrace.

--o0o—

FRIEND AT ALL TIMES

In darkness, I lost sight of You
and felt I was alone,
but deep inside, my spirit knew
I was not on my own.

The waters rose and strong floods beat
upon my troubled soul;
but waiting at Your mercy seat
was grace to make me whole.

The circumstances of my life
had changed so very much,
yet through it all You wanted to
bring comfort with Your touch.

I tried my best the load to carry,
foolishly I failed.
In weakness, I came to myself,
perplexed with my travail.

Why did I take so long to run
into Your hiding place,
when there to reassure me was
the beauty of Your face?

Jesus, You're so precious, waiting
patiently with love.
When often I despair of me,
You help me rise above.

Your love lifts me to higher heights
to focus on the goal,
for Jesus, You're my heart's desire,
the Lover of my soul.

I thank You for the hills and mountains
and the valleys too.
I'm thankful, Lord, for everything
that You have brought me through.

I thank You for the comfort of
Your presence deep within.
You help me fight the battles and
the victory to win.

I know my words are not enough
to give You all the praise.
O may the life I live for You
exalt Your Name always.

--oOo—

FOR YESTERDAY

For yesterday ..
I thank You, Lord.
There were years that seemed
just like a dream.
There were life-changing scenes.
But I've come to know
that You allowed me to go
through that maze, those difficult days,
You were there always.
You helped me grow,
You kept me strong -
like a tree amidst the storms.
You had hopes for me
when the future I couldn't see.
When I despaired, so misty was the view -
until I saw You,
looking down from heaven
showing You care.
Nothing compares
with Your love.
You saw my heart
and picked me up.
I owe everything to You.
For all You've done for me,
I'm grateful.
Lord … I thank You.

--o0o--

JUST WANT TO SAY THANKS

I looked through the window of life each day,
when the burdens were great and I hardly could pray.
If someone would ask of me how I fared,
with an answer, I'd smile, but I just couldn't share.

When the tears wouldn't cease and I felt I had failed,
You came through with peace, Your kindness prevailed.
You lifted me, Lord, and helped me to stand
on a rock, and You sheltered me there with Your hand.

Your Holy Spirit brought comfort and peace;
in the midst of my sorrow, and gave me relief
of the pain and the anguish that weighed like a stone.
You always were there, I was never alone.

O Jesus, I love You, I love You so much!
So precious to me is Your comforting touch.
Your wonderful peace You always impart;
just want to say "Thanks", from a grateful heart.

--o0o—

PERFECT ONE

You opened the door of life to me,
Your light of love shone through.
You offered me a hand to hold
and peace I never knew.

Never before could I have dreamt
that love like Yours existed,
but on the day that You came in,
I knew I was accepted.

Deep down within my heart is stored
a well of thanks and praise
that rises up when I think about
the wonder of Your ways.

The Perfect Shepherd You have been,
I've seen Your hand of care.
The Perfect Friend in everything,
Who's present everywhere.

The Perfect Light along my path,
the One Who guides my way;
the Perfect Source of strength and hope,
through each and every day.

Without You Jesus in my life,
I'd never have made it through;
for Yours is the love that stands the test,
it's perfect, pure and true.

I pray this love will shine, O Lord,
so someone else may see
that there is life, that there is hope
in You eternally.

--oOo--

POTTER

Thank You, Lord,
for Your arms of love
all around us,
shaping us
for heaven
above.
On solid ground
You keep our feet
as we walk life's street.
As a potter works with clay,
every day, You're working to
melt and mold us, till Your perfect
will unfolds; refining, till at last we're
shining, as gold. Help us, Lord, to
understand. Let this piece of clay, I pray,
be a useful vessel in Your hand,
surrendered and transformed
by Your pure and
holy love.

--o0o--

AT THE END OF THE DAY

At the end of the day,
when skies are dark,
in the quiet of night,
as silence fills the air;
before dreams
are deep as the ocean,
forgotten at dawn;
let's remember,
let's give thanks
to our Father, God;
always watching over us,
night and day -
never slumbering,
never sleeping;
always listening
for our prayer;
always being there,
our burdens to bear,
His love to share.
Thank You, Lord
for Your tender care
always.

--oOo—

Chapter 4

Loving Memories

Devotional Thoughts

Most of us have experienced loss and bereavement. Throughout life, we have moments when the memories come flooding back. Appreciation of all that our loved ones were to us is something that will live on and is another reason to be forever grateful.

Through faith in Christ, we can rejoice in the precious promise of scripture that we will meet our loved ones again.

"For the Lord Himself shall descend from heaven
with a shout, with the voice of the archangel,
and with the trump of God:
and the dead in Christ shall rise first:
Then we which are alive and remain shall be caught up
together with them in the clouds, to meet the Lord in the air:
and so shall we ever be with the Lord"
(1 Thessalonians 4:16-17 KJV)

BEYOND THE SUNSET

The night was long and hope held on
for morning light to shine;
the darkness passed and paved the way,
but then arrived the time.

The Bright and Morning Star reached out
His tender hands of love,
a precious soul to welcome to
His heavenly home above.

The years of life seemed like a day
of memories to keep.
For now your loved one, tired and worn,
has entered into sleep.

Beyond the sunset, there is rest
and everlasting peace;
the light of glory ever shines,
where life will never cease.

To all who place their faith in Christ,
God's promises stand sure.
One day we'll all be together again,
in life forevermore.

Take courage now and as the future
in your life unfolds,
keep treasuring the memories,
for they are more than gold.

--oOo—

A MEMORY SOMEWHERE

There must be a memory somewhere
deep down within my soul;
I just cannot recall it.
I was too young to know.
A babe was I, back then,
too young to realise
my mother had departed -
she lost the fight of life.

Her face I can't remember,
I cannot visualise.
I only have a picture
to place before my eyes.
I've missed the years of bonding,
of a mother's tender touch;
of all that could have been,
I've missed her very much.

But I'm so glad that one day
the time is coming when
we'll be together with loved ones,
when Christ shall come again.
No more a distant memory,
her face again I'll see;
my joy shall be complete when I
behold my dear Mummy.

--oOo--

PRECIOUS MEMORIES

Precious memories never fade,
within my heart, they'll always be;
although long years have passed and gone,
a treasure was my dad to me.
The only parent I ever knew,
he was, to me, just like a friend;
his tender love always shone through
in things he did, right 'til the end.

Through toil and hardship he pressed on,
through rain and sun, through day and night;
he did his best, though the road was long,
to see that we would be all right.
Now older and wiser, I can see
that love endures forever strong -
it binds together a family,
it never fails but marches on.

Thank you Lord for my loving Dad;
and for all the things he was to me;
now at rest within Your arms
I'm glad one day his face I'll see.

--o0o--

MY SWEET SISTER

The memories of all she was to me
are treasures deep within that soothe the pain.
The beauty of her kind and tender heart,
like roses, always bloomed in cold or rain.

She fought the battle of life with inner strength
and brought a ray of sunshine with her smile.
Her faith in God sustained her in the storms;
she came through many a time, despite the trials.

I often wished I could have done much more,
at times when she was in and out of care,
but I thank God for all the years she lived -
for precious thoughts of her are always near.

One day in heaven, we all shall meet again,
where joys abound and we will never part.
I know she's safe within the arms of Love;
'til then I'll treasure her within my heart.

--o0o—

Chapter 5

Divine Creation

Devotional Thoughts

We only need to look around us to see the awesomeness and wonder of God's creation. His glory is revealed in the heavens and throughout the whole earth.

"For the invisible things of Him from the creation of the world are clearly seen, being understood by the things that are made, even His eternal power and Godhead."
(Romans 1:20a KJV)

"For by Him were all things created, that are in heaven, and that are in earth, visible and invisible, whether they be thrones, or dominions, or principalities, or powers: all things were created by Him, and for Him:"
(Colossians 1:16 KJV)

MORNING TWEETS!

I hear them in the morning when I rise,
before the slightest glimpse of light appears.
A moment longer I must close my eyes;
their song so sweetly falls upon my ears.

The music of their tweets now fills the air.
Could man himself create a sweeter sound?
In silence I just want to linger there
and relish as the symphony abounds.

I know this time of bliss can only last
a while, for soon demands call me away.
But I'll not hurry till the time is past,
for now the sounds of birdsong bid me stay.

So tweet and chirp my friends, for I am blessed
to hear your song as I arise from rest!

--o0o--

HEAVEN AND EARTH DECLARE

His eyes are on the sparrow and
His strong wind turns the mills;
the silver and the gold are His
and cattle on a thousand hills.

He beautifies the lilies and
His rainbows grace the sky,
reminding all who dwell on earth
of His covenant on high.

Through trees that line the forests shine
the piercing rays of sun;
the depths of coral seas reveal
the wonders of the One

Whose hands uphold the universe
and all things by His power;
the One Whose love and grace are on
display each passing hour.

The heavens declare Your glory, Lord,
the sun, the moon and stars.
Creation tells the story of
how wonderful You are.

O precious Lord and Father,
One and only God, supreme,
Your love for all mankind is like
an ever-flowing stream.

For though You're high and mighty,
You look down in human hearts;
where sin has spoiled the picture,
there is hope for a brand new start.

How wonderful that through Your Son,
our Saviour, You should give
the hope of life eternally,
so man, through Him, can live.

There's none on earth like You, dear Lord,
Your power is divine.
Your love is inexplicable,
enduring for all time.

--o0o--

"The heavens declare the glory of God;
and the firmament sheweth His handiwork"
(Psalms 19:1 KJV)

EVERYWHERE

Sunset, golden skies,
glorious rays;
twilight greys
at the close of each day;

midnight,
shimmering stars,
mellow moonshine.

fresh dawn sunrise,
soft gentle breeze,
over housetops;
through trees,

dew drops like crystals;
skylarks' happy song;
brand new day,
breath of life.

Each day, each hour,
displaying God's power.
He is there
.. everywhere ..

permeating hidden places,
occupying open spaces,

realms of the deep,
distant shores,
galaxies, such mysteries.

Within and without,
all of creation,
beautiful art,
mankind in His heart.

In the atmosphere,
whether far or near;
never hid from His eyes
when we sit, when we rise;
every thought, He knows
everywhere we go.

His thoughts towards us
a treasure,
.. beyond measure ..
He seeks a place
in that special space
.. our hearts ..

Dear Lord,
help mankind to be aware
how much You care,
for You are
.. everywhere ..

"How marvellous,
O God, is Your love!"

--oOo--

(Based on Psalm 139)

BEHIND THE DESIGN

To every design,
there was a mind
working behind;
it played a part,
inspired the art
that touched a heart;

a meadow, a tree,
a big bumble bee,
the fish in the sea;
a sparrow on high,
scaling the sky
a bright butterfly;

a river, a spring,
water splashing,
so refreshing!
Radiant rays
on bright sunny days,
beautiful haze;

a sweet tortoiseshell,
a graceful gazelle,
looking so swell;
the crisp morning dew
as day starts anew,
refreshing view;

a beautiful dove,
a rainbow above,
symbol of love;
earth's grand design
came from a Mind
working behind;

and to work He went,
God omniscient,
precious moment;
right from the start,
God's perfect art
that touches our heart!

Earth's only Creator
and Originator,
there is none greater!
His the design,
His was the mind
working behind ..

…   the creation …
of the universe!

--o0o--

WHEN THE SUN SHINES

When the sun shines
it beautifies,
refreshing our eyes.

Like a gentle tide,
memories flow
of precious days gone by,
the growing years,
loved ones, special places,
precious moments,
different faces.

Joyful sounds abound as
children play, their day
full of new discoveries.

Hearts are cheered
and smiles appear
as grey gives way
to azure skies above
and all around us
glistens.

Love blossoms,
two hearts share;
fragrant scents
fills the air.

Radiant rays
beam through lofty
forests.

Warm crimson sunsets
close glorious days;

twilight haze
paves the way
for starlit skies.

Thank you
dear Lord
for the beautiful
gift of gold!

--oOo--

"Truly the light is sweet, and a pleasant thing it is
for the eyes to behold the sun:"
(Ecclesiastes 11: 7a KJV)

ABOUT THE AUTHOR

Christine V Mitchell was born in London, England. At the age of just 18 months, she experienced loss when her mother passed away. She and her sister lived in a children's home in the countryside, where they were well looked after. After 9 years of being without both parents, Christine and her sister returned to London to live with her loving father, Daniel McKenzie (now deceased).

The challenges of life never escaped her as, both in her youth and adulthood, she experienced the responsibilities of being a caregiver. She came to faith in Christ in her teens, which caused her to embark upon a spiritual journey where she found hope, true love, strength beyond her capacity to understand and a joy that she had never experienced before.

As a young adult, with a career in administration, her creativity blossomed and her skills as a musician and songwriter developed over the years. She now works alongside her wonderful husband, Pastor Frederick Mitchell, leading a warm fellowship of growing Christians and serving administratively also.

Within the last 10 years, Christine has been very inspired to write poetry. Her poems have helped bring hope and encouragement to others. Her heart is full and speaking the experiences of her personal relationship with God, and it gives her great joy to share her inspirational collection with the world. She is also the author of "Comfort and Hope" which follows this book.

Christine lives in London with her husband and together they have a wonderful family of 4 grown children (2 sons and 2 daughters), daughter-in-law and 2 grandchildren. If this poetry collection has been a blessing to you, please feel free to write and share. Christine would love to hear from you!

For further information,
(or if you would like to purchase a copy for a friend!) -

Visit Christine's website at:
www.expressionspoetry.com

Her books of poetry are available via:
www.amazon.com
www.amazon.co.uk
and other Amazon websites
or online retailers and bookstores.